Story Cards

Traditional Tales
Ages 8–12

WHITEHAWK PRIMARY SCHOOL

Written by
Lois Johnson

Published by
Hopscotch Educational Publishing Ltd
Unit 2
The Old Brushworks
56 Pickwick Road
Corsham
Wiltshire
SN13 9BX

01249 701701

© 2005 Hopscotch Educational Publishing

Written by Lois Johnson
Series design by Blade Communications
Illustrated by Debbie Clark
Printed by Cle-print

ISBN: 1-904307-87-6

Lois Johnson hereby asserts her moral right to be identified as the author of this work in accordance with the Copyright, Designs and Patents Act, 1988.

All rights reserved. This book is sold subject to the condition that it shall not, by way of trade or otherwise, be lent, hired out or otherwise circulated without the publisher's prior consent in any form of binding or cover other than that in which it is published and without a similar condition, including this condition, being imposed upon the subsequent purchaser.

No part of this publication may be reproduced, stored in a retrieval system, or transmitted, in any form or by any means, electronic, mechanical, photocopying, recording or otherwise, without the prior permission of the publisher, except where photocopying for educational purposes within the school or other educational establishment that has purchased this book is expressly permitted in the text.

Every effort has been made to trace the owners of copyright of material in this book and the publisher apologises for any inadvertent omissions. Any persons claiming copyright for any material should contact the publisher who will be happy to pay the permission fees agreed between them and who will amend the information in this book on any subsequent reprint.

Story Cards
Traditional Tales

CONTENTS

Introduction	4
Lesson 1	7
Lesson 2	8
Lesson 3	9
Lesson 4	11
Lesson 5	13
Further activities	15
Text 1: Jack and the Beanstalk	18
Text 2: The Seal Wife	24
Text 3: The Three Little Pigs	29
Planning sheets	30

Story Cards

INTRODUCTION

About the series

Story Cards is an exciting and innovative series of books and cards aimed at developing and enriching the storytelling and story-writing skills of children at Key Stages 1 and 2.

There are two books and card packs for Key Stage 1:
- Traditional Tales
- Fantasy

and four books and card packs for Key Stage 2:
- Myths and Legends
- Science Fiction
- Fantasy
- Traditional Tales

Each book and accompanying card pack aims to:
- support teachers by providing a wealth of interesting ideas for storytelling and story-writing lessons;
- reduce teachers' preparation time through the provision of differentiated activities and photocopiable resources;
- stimulate children's interest and enjoyment in storytelling and story-writing;
- develop children's speaking and writing skills through stimulating and purposeful activities that are fun to do.

Each book has an accompanying **CD-Rom** that contains all the graphic images contained in the corresponding card pack. These images can be saved on a computer and/or printed off. This is an excellent additional resource because it enables the teacher to create her own displays, posters, books and resources using professional-looking graphics.

About each book and card pack

There is one book and an accompanying pack of cards for each story genre (see above) at Key Stages 1 and 2.

Each book contains:
- background information about the writing genre;
- detailed lesson plans for using the cards to develop storytelling and story-writing skills;
- exemplar stories that are differentiated;
- differentiated planning sheets;
- further activities – a wealth of further ideas for using the cards for additional writing tasks as well as speaking and listening games and activities.

Each lesson plan includes differentiated tasks to take into account children of differing ability levels – thereby enabling all the children to work towards the intended learning objectives.

At Key Stage 2, the story cards are divided into six categories and these vary for each different story genre. For example, in the *Myths and Legends* pack they are:
- hero;
- quest;
- companion;
- item;
- setting;
- enemy.

Each category consists of six cards. For example, the enemy cards in the *Myths and Legends* pack feature a one-eyed giant, a many-headed beast, a troll, a huge serpent, a dragon and an evil knight.

Thus, by selecting just one card from each of the six categories, a complete story outline is created. By varying the cards used, a different outline can be created each time. The idea of giving the hero a companion and a special item to take on his quest is partly traditional but also, importantly, it allows the children to be more imaginative with their stories.

How to use the book and card pack

It is recommended that the teacher follows the lesson plans first, in order, from Lesson 1 through to Lesson 5. This ensures that the cards are introduced to the children in a structured way and that the teacher achieves confidence in using them as a basis for lesson planning.

After the lessons have been carried out, the children will have gained valuable knowledge about the particular writing genre as well as greater confidence in storytelling and -writing. To extend the life of the cards, the children can be encouraged to create their own cards to add to each category – or even make up their own complete set of cards to keep themselves.

The tasks in the further activities section can be used to extend and follow up the lessons. These activities are fun to do and will encourage the children to develop their speaking, listening and language skills.

About this book

This book forms part of the *Traditional Tales Story Cards* pack. It explains how to use the story cards for storytelling and story-writing activities. The book and card pack is intended for use with children in Key Stage 2. The lesson plans and activities contained in this book are adaptable enough to be used with children across the key stage because suggestions for manageable differentiation are included.

The lesson plans

The book contains five lesson plans. It is suggested that the lessons are followed in order because the intention is to introduce the children to traditional tales and then encourage them to write their own.

Each lesson plan contains:
- **Learning objectives**
  This outlines the learning objectives for the lesson.
- **Resources**
  This lists the resources needed to carry out the lesson.
- **What to do**
  This outlines the lesson in detail.
- **Ideas for differentiation**
  This gives suggestions for how the teacher might differentiate the main task in the lesson.
- **Plenary**
  This provides suggestions for the plenary session at the end of the lesson.

Exemplar texts

There are three exemplar stories provided in the book:
- Text 1 – Jack and the Beanstalk
- Text 2 – The Seal Wife
- Text 3 – The Three Little Pigs

The texts have been illustrated, making them suitable for the children to read and enjoy. You may like to enlarge them on an OHP or photocopy them for individual use. Text 3 is an example of a 'poor' piece of writing that the children are encouraged to improve.

Comic strip versions of texts 1 and 2 have also been included in order to provide differentiation. The teacher can choose to use these comic strip versions in different ways:
- to support less able children by providing them with a version they can read themselves;
- to use in future lessons to encourage the children to write comic strip versions of their own or well-known stories;
- to demonstrate how stories can be shortened and still retain meaning;
- to use as a model for a playscript;
- to provide ideas for creating picture-book versions of the story.

Planning sheets and additional resources

At the back of the book there are three planning sheets that are used as part of the lessons. The sheets are differentiated.

Further activities

This section of the book contains lots of ideas for the teacher to use the story cards in different ways and to develop the lesson plans further.

It contains:
- ten-minute speaking and listening activities – a collection of exciting ideas for using the story cards in a variety of games and activities;
- notes about storytelling;
- notes about drama;
- art and craft ideas;
- extended writing activities.

Story cards

The story cards consist of:

<u>Main characters</u> <u>Villains</u>
boy wicked stepmother
girl greedy queen
prince fierce king
princess ruthless lord
old man sly dwarf
old woman monstrous giant

<u>Animals</u> <u>Magical items</u>
pig sack
wolf tree
horse seeds
bird stick
bear key
frog potion

<u>Tales</u> <u>Settings</u>
find something cottage
lose something forest
be warned of something village
defeat someone castle
meet someone palace
wish for something river

CD-Rom

The graphics on the accompanying CD-Rom can be used in many different ways:
- to make large posters of each character/place in order to create an effective class display;
- to make a large class book of the stories;
- to make additional story cards;
- to create hanging mobiles for dramatic classroom displays;
- to make stick puppets (by gluing to stiff card) for dramatisation;
- to use as inspiration for the children to create their own characters/places/items.

Traditional tales – Background information

Traditional tales are stories that have been passed on as spoken tales from one generation to the next. They have been told and retold, sometimes with subtle changes woven into the story by the narrator. These stories were eventually written down in their many forms. The genre encompasses several types of story, including fairytales, folk tales and fables. Many of the themes of traditional tales appear across different cultures and numerous versions exist of each one. This is due to the origins of traditional tales being spoken as opposed to being recorded in a written form.

Fairytales encompass an element of magic or enchantment; for example, a prince turning into a frog in 'The Golden Ball', a pumpkin turned into a coach by a fairy godmother in 'Cinderella' and the magic beans that grow into a gigantic beanstalk in 'Jack and the Beanstalk'. Fairytales often begin with 'Once upon a time...' and usually end with everyone living happily ever after. Sometimes these stories also contain magical folk such as fairies or elves; for example, 'The Elves and the Shoemaker'.

Folk tales originate from a particular ethnic people and the oral tradition of these tales tells the story of their history, culture and superstitions. In some cultures these stories are still passed on orally rather than told in a written format. Folk tales usually have a simple plot concerning a theme or message.

Fables often feature a talking animal as the main character. This type of traditional tale teaches the reader a moral or lesson to be learned from their behaviour or actions. The most famous fables are those of Aesop, who is thought to have been a Greek slave who lived about 600BC. Aesop used animals to point out the errors in people's behaviour. His fables were translated into English by Sir Robert L'Estrange. Jean de la Fontaine, a French man, also wrote fables, but Aesop remains the most famous creator of fables and his name is almost synonymous with the genre.

Lesson 1

Learning objective

- To identify the key features of traditional tales.

Resources

- An enlarged copy of either Text 1 (pages 18–21) or Text 2 (pages 24–26)
- The *Traditional Tales Story Cards* pack

What to do

- Tell the children that over the next few lessons they are going to find out about traditional tales in order to write their own. Explain that traditional tales are stories that have been passed on from one generation to the next, originally by storytelling. They often feature talking creatures or animals acting like people. Sometimes there is an element of magic, such as turning one thing into another, and almost anything is possible.

- Many different types of story come under the genre of traditional tales. Do the children know of any? Discuss their ideas and confirm examples such as 'The Three Little Pigs', 'Jack and the Beanstalk' and 'Rumpelstiltskin'. Explain that we sometimes come across different versions of the same story. Other examples of traditional tales are tales from other countries that share the same features and are often basically the same story but with different characters. Say that another type of traditional tale is a fable. This type of story shows the reader that there are consequences for certain types of behaviour and thus fables contain a moral.

- Begin to share the story with the children, pausing to discuss events and key features. Can they easily identify who the main character in the story will be? Ask them if they think the task the main character has to complete will be successful. Finish reading the story and, after discussion, ask them to tell you what they think makes a traditional tale different from other stories. Discuss their ideas and then make a note of the key features of traditional tales; for example, the main character has to complete a task to get his reward, there is often an element of magic that helps the main character and the story usually has a happy ending.

- Explain to the children that in fairytales we often find certain words or phrases used at the beginning and the end of a story, such as 'Once upon a time...' and 'They all lived happily ever after.' These phrases help us to identify a traditional tale. Can they think of examples of phrases that are repeated throughout a story; for example, 'I'll huff and I'll puff and I'll blow your house down,' and 'Fee, fi, fo, fum'? These sayings are repeated by the characters and this is another feature of traditional tales – phrases, sayings or descriptions used repeatedly for effect.

- Introduce the story cards. Explain how the cards represent each of the story components (main character, animal, villain, magical item, setting and tale). Show them some of the cards. For example, look at the tale cards. Explain that each of these cards represents a different story idea. Ask for ideas on how the tales could be developed and what kind of complications could arise.

- Divide the children into groups and give each group one of the villain cards. Ask them to discuss the character on the card so that they can share their ideas with the rest of the class.

Ideas for differentiation

Ability group 1
Ask these children to think of as many different ways as they can in which their villain could hinder or harm the main character. Can they think of special powers or qualities their villain might have and how they could be used?

Ability group 2
Ask these children to think of as many ways as they can to describe their villain and how he or she would cause problems or trouble for the main character. In addition, does he or she have any special powers or magic that would help and can they think of a suitable short description of the villain?

Ability group 3
Ask these children to think of accurate and interesting descriptions of their villain as for the previous group, as well as to try to think of a phrase to be repeated throughout the story to identify them, such as a short description or something the villain says.

Allow enough time for the groups to share their ideas on their villain card. Note: children within each group do not have to agree on one choice of description. The more ideas for each card the better as this will ultimately allow them to produce more individual stories. Invite children from each group to share their thoughts, acting out their villain character.

Plenary

- Ask the children what makes a traditional tale different from other types of story. Can they remember the key features that make up this kind of story? Can they remember the definitions from the beginning of the lesson?

Lesson 2

Learning objectives

- To identify the difference between the first and third persons.
- To create brief descriptions.

Resources

- The *Traditional Tales Story Cards* pack

What to do

- Ask the children what they can remember about the previous lesson on traditional tales. Can they remember any of the key features? Discuss their ideas and remind them about the possible use of magic, talking animals, a task that must be completed and a happy ending.

- Remind the children about the main character in the story shared in the previous lesson. Explain that this story is told from the main character's viewpoint and so it is written in something called the third person – using the character's name and 'he' (or 'she' if Text 2 was used in the previous lesson). Ask the children if they know what the first person is. Discuss their ideas and confirm that 'I' and 'we' are first person. Explain that most stories are written in the third person.

- Ask the children to work with a partner for a few minutes to see if they can think of examples when they could use the first person. After allowing a few minutes' discussion, ask them to share their ideas with the rest of the class. Confirm that diaries, letters and some stories are written from the first person viewpoint but also, importantly, in stories written in the third person, when the characters speak, their dialogue is in the first person. For example, Jack's mother said, 'We have no food and no money, Jack. We'll have to sell the cow at the market.' 'OK,' Jack replied. 'I'll go straight away.' This makes their dialogue more realistic. When we talk we do not usually refer to ourselves by our name; instead we use 'I'. In this example, Jack's mother uses the plural form of the first person – 'we' – and Jack uses the singular – 'I'.

- Remind the children about the story cards they shared in the previous lesson. Tell them that in the next lesson they are going to use the cards to help them plan their own traditional tale. Explain that before they do this, they are going to explore some more ideas about the items on the story cards – each of the characters and items on the cards has their own special features and characteristics that add detail and interest to a story. Show the children the character cards.

- Ask the children to work with a partner for a few minutes and come up with a short sentence about one of the characters (third person). Then they imagine they are that character (first person). How would the sentence change? Discuss their ideas.

- Now show them the animal cards. Ask them to decide whether the animals can talk and behave in other human-like ways or whether they are more like real animals. Explain that in some traditional tales there are no human characters at all. These story cards use both humans and animals to give them more choice when they plan their story.

- Ask the children to work with their partner for a few minutes. Each pair is to think of a brief description of one of the animals. Ask them to share their ideas with the rest of the class.

- Divide the children into the same groups as in the previous lesson and give them one card from each of the character and animal categories. Ask them to work individually or in pairs to make up special characteristics or features of their cards. Tell them that at the end of the lesson they will be expected to share their ideas with the rest of the class.

Ideas for differentiation

Ability group 1
Ask these children to decide whether the animal on their card will help the main character in completing the task or try to stop him or her? Does the animal have any magical powers; for example, can it speak?

Ability group 2
Ask these children to decide whether the animal is a helpful creature, working with the main character, or whether it is working with/for the villain. Will it try to prevent the main character from being successful? How does the animal behave?

Ability group 3
These children could be challenged by asking them to think of a phrase or group of phrases which they could use to describe the main character or animal or which could be spoken repeatedly for effect by either the character or the animal. For example, in The Three Little Pigs, much of the story is told by repeated sayings.
The Wolf – 'I'll huff and I'll puff...' and so on.
The Pigs – 'Not by the hair of my chinny, chin chin.'

Plenary

- Bring the children back together. Ask each group to present their ideas to the rest of the class. Can the others suggest further ideas?

Lesson 3

Learning objectives

- To recognise the beginning, middle and ending of a story.
- To identify what happens in the main part of a story.
- To plan a story.

Resources

- The story planning sheets (pages 30–32)
- An enlarged version of Planning sheet 2 (page 31)
- An enlarged copy of either Text 1 (pages 18–21) or Text 2 (pages 24–26)
- The *Traditional Tales Story Cards* pack

What to do

- Remind the children about the traditional tale from Lesson 1 and read the story again from the enlarged version. Explain that the story has a beginning, a middle and an ending. Ask the children for ideas on identifying each of the three parts. For example, 'What does the first part tell us?' Expect answers from the children such as, 'It tells us who is in the story (characters).' Ask 'Does it tell us where the story is set (setting) or does this come later?' and 'Are we given any ideas about what might be going to happen (plot/action)?'

- Discuss the children's suggestions then confirm their ideas – the main character (or characters) is usually introduced in the beginning. In addition, we are sometimes told about the place (setting) where the story starts and given some idea of what the story may be about (plot). The middle of the story is all about how the main character attempts the task. This is where most of the action takes place. Finally, look at the ending of the story. Here the main character is successful and everyone lives happily ever after.

- Tell the children that they can use the story cards to help them plan their own story with a beginning, middle and ending. Explain that you are going to show them how to do this.

- Lay the cards out within their categories (character, animal, villain, magical item, setting and tale) and select one card from each type. Hold up the individual cards as they are chosen and ask a child to describe them for the rest of the class.

- For example, cards chosen could be: main character – boy; animal – bird; tale – warning; magical item – seeds; setting – river; villain – greedy queen.

- Begin to plan the story from the chosen story cards, using the enlarged copy of Planning sheet 2. Explain that there are many ways to plan a story and that some children will be using a different planning sheet, but they will still be recording the same details. Ensure they all understand why it is important to plan a story first rather than just starting to write one. Explain that it is too much information to try to keep in our heads, so we need to write down all our good ideas. Remind them that when they are filling in a story planning sheet they do not need to write in full sentences – they can just use words and phrases. These will be reminders of what to include when they begin to write the story.

- On the enlarged planning sheet fill in the details of the main character: boy – give him a name (for example, Tom); tale: warning (for example, Tom has been warned not to go somewhere). And so on. When all the above information has been recorded on the planning sheet, move on to adding some of the detail that will be used when writing the story.

- Ask the children if they can remember what should be included at the beginning of a story. Reinforce their ideas of introducing the main character and the tale. Remind them that Tom has been warned not to do something; however, this is usually exactly what the main character does! Look at the chosen cards again and ask the children for suggestions about what the warning could be. Ask them to work with a partner for a few minutes to discuss their ideas and then share them with the rest of the class. Add these details to the planning sheet so that the theme for a tale is being built up. For example, 'Tom's mother forbids him from going near palace of greedy queen.'

- Move on to the middle part, adding outline details to build up a plot. For example, 'Queen has a secret. Villagers are poor and hungry but queen won't give money or food. All she cares about is gold and jewels and looking beautiful.'

- Tell the children that all the items have magical powers. Ask them for ideas about what kind of magic the seeds could have. Could this be the greedy queen's secret?

- After taking suggestions from the children, choose the most appropriate and annotate the enlarged planning sheet accordingly. For example, the magic seeds could grow into trees of gold with jewels hanging from the branches like fruit.

- Remind the children of the setting – river. Ask them for ideas on how this could be used, for example, 'greedy queen's palace on other side of river'.

- Take ideas from the children about how the villain, the greedy queen, will try to defeat Tom. For example, she has soldiers guarding the river to stop anyone trying to cross.

- Remind the children about the animal on the chosen card – a bird. Ask them for ideas about how the bird could help Tom to get to the palace without crossing the river. For example, 'Tom knew the only way he could get to the palace gardens was by digging a tunnel under the river so the soldiers wouldn't see him.' But how would he know which direction to follow? 'The bird flies across the river and sits in one of the golden trees. Bird sings sweetest, loudest song. Tom follows sound.'

- Complete the planning sheet. Check that all the elements from the story cards have been included and that there is sufficient detail on the planning sheet to make an exciting story.

- Divide the children into the same groups as the previous lesson and give them the same villain, character and animal cards they have already discussed. In addition, give each group a setting, magical item and tale card so that they now have a complete set of six story cards.

Ideas for differentiation

The three planning sheets are already differentiated and give structure to the planning process. Encourage the children to use their imagination when planning their stories so that their writing creates a story unique to them, showing their individuality.

Ability group 1
Give these children a copy of Planning sheet 1. This gives additional support in that it contains a word bank of basic key words for the children to use. There is space for them to note down suitable words or phrases that they intend using in their stories. Ask them to plan their own story outline, referring to the story cards as necessary to prompt ideas.

Ability group 2
Give these children a copy of Planning sheet 2. This outlines the key features the children need to include and gives them reminders of the kinds of words they could use in their story. Ask the children to plan their own story outline, including ideas for descriptions/action as they do so. The story cards are available for them to remind them of all the things they are going to include and to encourage them to add descriptions.

Ability group 3
Give these children a copy of Planning sheet 3. This is an advanced planning sheet and features a noticeably different layout from the other two planning sheets. This is to highlight the build-up of drama and conflict within a story and thus encourage the children to remember this when planning their own writing.

Ask the children to plan their own story outline with the additional challenge of using more conflict in their story. For example, can they invent a second villain for the main character to defeat? Or could the task be more complicated than it appeared? Perhaps, after the main character succeeds, the completed task creates a further problem?

Plenary

- Ask the children the following kinds of questions to reinforce the learning objectives focused on in the lesson: What are the three parts to every story? How can they be identified? Why have we planned our stories?

- Confirm the idea that if we didn't plan and just started to write a story it would be easy to miss something out and then the story might not make sense. Remind them that planning their stories gives them an opportunity to add interest and excitement.

- Invite children into a 'hot seat' to share their story plans. Can they imagine they are the main character? What is their tale? Where are they going? What is it like? What can they see? How do they feel?

Lesson 4

Learning objectives

- To identify the use of pronouns and understand their function.
- To ensure nouns and pronouns are used effectively.
- To write a story beginning.

Resources

- Children's story plans from previous lesson
- Teacher's enlarged planning sheet from previous lesson
- Enlarged version of Text 3 (page 29)
- Copies of Text 3 for the children
- The *Traditional Tales Story Cards* pack

What to do

- Remind the children of the traditional tale shared previously and ask them whether the character's name is always used when they are referred to or whether sometimes they are called 'he' or 'she'. Explain that it is better to use a pronoun to identify someone instead of constantly using the character's name.

- Read the following example: 'Jack's mother asked him to take the cow to sell at the market.' Explain that if 'him' was not used to replace 'Jack' in this sentence, it would be: 'Jack's mother asked Jack to take the cow to sell at the market.' This sounds clumsy and repetitive, especially if done throughout a whole story.

- Explain that we can also use the pronoun 'it' or 'them' in place of a thing or things. Discuss the need for a balance and remind the children that if all the nouns are replaced the text can become confusing. For example: 'They were very sad because they had none of it. So she asked him to take it there and sell it. But he met him who gave him them for it.' This should be written: 'Jack and his mother were very sad because they had no money. So she asked him to take the cow to the market and sell it. But Jack met an old man who gave him beans for the cow'. This is a better balance between nouns and pronouns.

- Remind the children of the use of the first person pronouns; for example, 'I' and 'we' and ask them if they can remember when these are especially useful in story writing. Confirm their ideas, reinforcing the importance of using 'I' and 'we' in direct speech because that is how characters refer to themselves.

- Tell the children that they are now going to share a text that needs correcting. The first part contains no pronouns and in the second part there are too many. Read out the story from an enlarged copy of Text 3. Provide them with copies of the story. Ask them to correct this text so that there is a balance between nouns and pronouns and the extract makes more sense. After allowing a few minutes, discuss their editing of the text.

- Remind the children about Tom's story that was planned as a class in the previous lesson. Explain that they are now going to think about writing the beginning of the story. Display the enlarged planning sheet. Ask them what should be included in the beginning. Look at the story cards again to remind them of all the elements they need to include in their stories.

- Ask the children for ideas about how this story could begin. Confirm their ideas that the main character, Tom, should be introduced at the beginning, plus details about his task. Take suggestions from the children about how this could actually be worded. For example:

Once upon a time, in a land far away, lived a boy called Tom and his mother. They were very poor and always hungry. Every night Tom went to bed with an empty stomach and dreamed of huge tables overflowing with food. He was a hard-working boy but no matter how much he worked there was never enough money because the greedy queen who ruled the land took almost all their money in taxes.

The greedy queen was powerful and vain. All she cared about was money and jewels to make herself look more beautiful. But she was so greedy that she would rather the villagers starve than share her wealth with them. Rumours spread throughout Tom's village that the queen even had magic seeds that grew into golden trees laden with precious jewels. But no-one knew for sure. Anyone who dared to cross the river to her palace to find out was never seen again. Every time Tom left the cottage his mother called, 'Stay away from the river, Tom.' And Tom always replied, 'Yes, Mother.'

- Ask the children to check that this would be a suitable beginning. Confirm that the main character has been introduced, plus his tale.

- Tell the children that they are now going to use their planning sheets to write the beginning of their own traditional tale.

Ideas for differentiation

All the groups should have the story cards available to remind them of the elements they are to include and to give them ideas for adding extra detail.

Ability group 1
Ask this group to write the beginning of their own story, remembering to use any especially good words or phrases they have included on their planning sheets, plus appropriate words chosen from those supplied in the word bank. Remind them to vary between using their character's name and 'he' or 'she', instead of simply repeating the name.

Ability group 2
Ask this group to write the beginning of their story. Ask them to choose words carefully to create a strong image and make their writing interesting. Remind the children that a good beginning makes a reader want to read on.

Ability group 3
Ask this group to write the beginning of their story. They should remember to include detailed descriptions. Challenge – to make their story openings interesting and their dialogue realistic, can they use a repeated phrase to identify their character, animal or villain? For example, 'I'll huff and I'll puff...' They learned about phrases, sayings or descriptions used repeatedly for effect in Lesson 1.

Plenary

- Ask the children to share their opening sentences and paragraphs. What do the others think? Are the beginnings interesting? Discuss ideas for how their stories could move on to the middle part.

Lesson 5

Learning objectives

- To write the middle and ending of a story.
- To edit a story, ensuring punctuation is used effectively.

Resources

- Children's story plans and beginnings from previous lesson
- Teacher's enlarged planning sheet from previous lesson
- The *Traditional Tales Story Cards* pack

What to do

- ❑ Tell the children that in this lesson they are going to concentrate on story middles and endings. Share ideas for what should be included in the middle of a traditional tale – the main character must encounter a problem and thwart the villain, but we know he will succeed and the story will have a happy ending.

- ❑ Show the children the enlarged planning sheet and read out the ideas for the middle of the story. Explain that they are going to help write the middle part. Remind them about the beginning written in the previous lesson and ask them to work with a partner for a few minutes to think of ideas for how the story could continue. Discuss their suggestions.

- ❑ Begin to write down examples so the text resembles something like:

One night, as Tom lay in bed, all he could think about was food. He was so hungry he just couldn't sleep, no matter how hard he tried. Finally, he decided to go for a walk and it was such a beautiful, moonlit night that he wandered to the riverbank and saw the stars reflected in the water.

- ❑ Pause and ask the children if they can hear the punctuation in the sentences. Expect them to answer that they can't. Ask them to listen very carefully and read the last few sentences out loud but without any punctuation – 'One night as Tom lay in bed all he could think about was food he was so hungry he just couldn't sleep no matter how hard he tried finally he decided to go for a walk and it was such a beautiful moonlit night that he wandered to the riverbank and saw the stars reflected in the water'.

- ❑ Then read it again, pausing for the punctuation and ask them again. Explain that they need to include the correct punctuation when writing their stories to help their reader follow the story and to make sure their writing makes sense.

- ❑ Continue writing the story, using the ideas from the planning sheet. For example:

Tom was so tired he fell asleep under an old oak tree. As the sun rose, he was woken by the song of a bird sitting in the branches of the tree. He looked across the river and saw the turrets of the palace rising up behind the high walls surrounding it. Tom remembered the story about the queen's magic seeds. If the trees inside the palace walls really were made of gold and laden with precious jewels, all he would need was one seed and he and his mother would never be hungry again. As he looked at the river and listened to the sweet song of the bird, Tom began to think of a plan.

- ❑ Ask the children what Tom will do next. Remind them of the story plan about Tom digging a tunnel under the river and share their suggestions. Discuss the possibilities and, taking the most suitable suggestions, finish the story.

- ❑ Tell the children that they will now finish writing their own traditional tale. They will have their planning sheets to remind them of their ideas so far.

Ideas for differentiation

Ability group 1
Ask the children to read the beginning of their story from the previous lesson and then continue by writing the middle and ending, ensuring they have included details from each of the story cards. They should include as many of the given words from the word bank as possible. When their story is complete, ask them to read it through again from the beginning, checking their punctuation to ensure it flows and makes sense.

Ability group 2
Ask the children to continue writing their stories, using their planning sheets for guidance and choosing words for emphasis and detail. After completion, the children should edit their story, improving the descriptions and checking their punctuation. The children could share their stories with a partner to highlight any particularly strong or weak areas and then work on these specific parts.

Ability group 3
Ask the children to continue writing their stories, using their planning sheets as reminders. Ask them to be selective in their choice of words so that they create stories in the style of a traditional tale, using repeated phrases, if possible. The children should ensure they have written in paragraphs and that their stories have a clear beginning, a build of action/excitement in the middle and a suitably happy ending.

Plenary

- Invite the children to share their stories with the rest of the class. Their stories can be assessed for key features and the children could be encouraged to think of their stories from a different viewpoint. How would the story change if it was told from the villain's point of view instead of the main character's? Can the children think of other ways in which their stories could have evolved?

Further activities

In addition to the series of writing lessons featured in this teacher's guide, the story cards may be used for many different types of activity, ranging from enhancing speaking and listening skills to expanding the children's writing skills in extended writing sessions. Here follow some ideas you can try out.

Ten-minute speaking and listening activities

Encouraging the children to discuss the story cards will enhance and expand their vocabulary. By using this kind of activity as a whole class activity, those children whose own vocabulary range is poor will have access to a wider range of descriptive words and phrases than they would normally use themselves. This will encourage them to extend their own vocabulary, both spoken and written.

Who/what is it?
- The children can work in either small groups or pairs. One child selects a card from the story cards pack and describes what the character/setting/magical item/animal/villain looks like in as much detail as possible without showing the card to the others. The other children can ask three questions before trying to guess the identity of the card chosen.

Naming game
- Ask the children to sit in a circle. The story cards are placed face down in the centre of the circle. One child selects a card and says one word about the character/animal/villain on the card. The card is then passed to the next child who says a different word. This continues round the circle, each child having to think up a new word to describe the card (for example, if the pig card is chosen – snout, grunt, squeal, tail, trotters, sty and so on).

- How far round the circle can they go before the children run out of new words? The next person then picks up a new card and the game begins again. Try to play the game as quickly as possible to keep the rhythm and momentum going.

Whose story is it?
- The children should be encouraged to share their creativity with others, either within groups or the whole class. Hot-seating is a particularly useful way to make the children aware of the main character's emotions and how they could change throughout the story; for example, excitement at the beginning, fear as he tries to defeat the villain, pride as he returns from a successful task and so on.

- Either working in groups or as a whole class activity, ask a child to select one of the tales cards. The child should imagine they are about to begin that tale and they describe how they are feeling. Are they nervous, afraid, anxious? Are they eager to be off on their adventure or worried about what they may encounter? Do they think their feelings would change as the story progresses?

- A second child is then asked to imagine they are the mother or father of the first child. They have to tell the others how they are feeling. Are they worried or are they feeling proud, or both?

- A third child could become the adversary the main character will meet, the villain. How do they feel about being defeated by this character? By discussing various characters' emotions the children will gain an understanding that sometimes feelings are not clear cut. Often people feel a mixture of conflicting emotions. It is useful to remember to tell the audience how a character is feeling in both verbal storytelling and story-writing.

- Another valuable aspect of this activity is that it allows the children to consider and experience the story from different perspectives.

Experts
- Ask the child(ren) to select a card and make up as much information about it as possible – making them an expert on that magical item/animal/setting. The experts can then be questioned by the others. The idea of this activity is for the experts to give the impression that they know absolutely everything there is to know through their manner and confidence in answering.

Why? Because…
- This activity could be carried out in small groups or as a circle game. A child selects a card. The next child asks a 'Why?' question; for example, 'Why is he smiling?' The person who selected the card (or the next person in the circle) has to make up a convincing answer to the question – 'He is smiling because…' The next child asks a different 'Why?' question and so on until no more 'Why?' questions can be thought of and a different card can be selected.

Chain story
- Set the cards out face down in their groups. Start the story off. 'Once upon a time there was (select a character card) who was very (describe the character). One day he sets off to explore (a child selects a setting card and continues the story).' The story continues until a card from each category has been selected.

Character CVs
- The character and villain cards are placed face down in their groups. A child selects a card and begins to make up a CV for that character. You could provide a framework for this activity so that each child in the group suggests one part of the CV (for example; name, address, childhood achievements, qualifications, special skills, previous jobs, hobbies/interests) or each child can make up the whole CV themselves. This activity could also be a written task.

Magical items
- Divide the children into small groups of five or six. Remind them that the story included a magical item. Ask them to imagine they are the main character and to think of a special magical item they might find. The children take it in turns to assume the role of the main character and give the group three clues as to what their special item is. Whoever guesses correctly is the next character.

- Ask the children to think what kind of special powers their magical item could have. How would they use these powers?

Storytelling

- Stories from around the world were originally told by word of mouth. Storytelling is a valuable skill which allows children the freedom to be creative with their imagination without the constraints of having to write their ideas down and worry about such things as spelling, punctuation, grammar and so on. The children should be encouraged to listen carefully to each other's stories as much as possible. In this way they share good practices and enhance their own skills and learning.

- Children who are not the most able story writers in the class may be adept at telling stories, especially after 'playing' with the story cards which gives their imagination a starting point from which they can explore and develop further.

Drama

- The previous ten-minute activities could lead on to drama sessions, either with groups of children acting out their own story or, if a longer-term project, the children under your guidance could merge several of the stories to make a longer, action-packed dramatic adventure.

- In addition to acting out their stories, it would be appropriate for the children to look at the differences that need to be taken into account when writing a play as opposed to a story. They should identify how a playscript is set out and discuss the need to include stage directions, acts and scenes. Share ideas with the children on how the actors will ensure the audience knows exactly where they are and what is happening.

- Using an agreed class story (either your story developed in the writing modelling sessions, or a combination of some of the children's), divide the children into groups to work on different scenes so that a complete play is written. Discuss the possible need for a narrator, or will the characters' words keep the audience informed? Alternatively, the children could work on an extract of their own story, perhaps just writing a short scene. This gives the children the opportunity to think of their story beyond the written page. Ensure the correct conventions are followed when writing drama, including layout and format.

Art and craft

Books
- After completing their stories, the children could make either their own individual books or, by including all the stories, a class book for display in the classroom, illustrating them as appropriate.

- The children could make a comic strip version of their story. Remind them to use speech and thought bubbles. Short sentences can be used to describe the setting. Much of the detail will be seen in the pictures so there is no need for long descriptions. In this type of story, the choice of words is not as important, as the story relies heavily on the illustrations carrying the reader forward.

Display
- If the children's stories are not made into books then they would be ideal material to form the basis of a display. Using the illustrations of the characters, villains and settings from the story cards to form the basis of their ideas, the children could make their own artwork to enhance the display and make it an eye-catching feature of the classroom.

Maps

- A map incorporating all the different settings as shown on the story cards, showing their individual features, could be incorporated into the class display featuring the children's stories. If set out on a grid, the map would make an excellent maths resource, showing coordinates for each tale, plus, if the map was large enough, details such as where certain events took place, where the main characters lived, where the villains were encountered and so on could be included. Can the children plot the various adventures of each of the main characters on the maps using the coordinates as reference points so that others can follow their paths?

Additional cards

❐ The children can create their own set of traditional tale story cards either individually or working in small groups with each child designing one card of each type so that together they make one set. These cards could be used in later storytelling/writing sessions or in the extended story writing ideas.

Extended writing activities

Sequel

❐ The children could write another tale for their character, by either changing one or two of the story cards and seeing how it would change their original story, or replacing certain story cards with their own ideas. Can they think of additional hazards the main character could encounter? What would happen if the animal was different. How would this affect the story? Or if the magical item was different? Their character could encounter a different villain or several different ones. Will he or she still succeed?

Revenge!

❐ Ask the children if they can think of what would happen if, after the main character's success, the villain returned to seek his or her revenge. The more the children can be encouraged to think about their stories and the possibilities for different ways the story line could go, the wider the expansion of their imagination and the more creative their ideas and vocabulary will become.

Twist in the tale

❐ Encourage the children to rewrite a traditional tale but with a twist. For example; perhaps, in The Three Little Pigs, the wolf could be the main character – after all, he's only trying to find a meal. Or are there three little wolves and one big, bad pig and this time it is the pig who is after the three little wolves? Look again at Jack and the Beanstalk. Try telling the story from the giant's point of view – he was living quite happily in his castle at the top of the beanstalk before Jack came along. How does he feel about having his belongings stolen by a thief? Try looking at the well-known traditional tales and imagining the story being told from a different perspective.

Animal world

❐ Using the story cards as a starting point, consider how the tales would change if the animals were the main characters instead of the people. Many traditional tales feature no people at all. Encourage the children to think of story ideas using the animal cards as the main characters, either without any human element or with the human characters playing a secondary role. Could any of the animals be used in the role of villain? Which of them would be most suited and what would their evil characteristics be?

TEXT 1
Jack and the Beanstalk

Once upon a time there was a poor woman who had a son called Jack. They lived in a humble cottage on the edge of a village. Their most precious possession was a cow called Buttercup that gave the richest, creamiest milk in all the land. Jack and his mother made some of the milk into butter and cheese to sell at the market.

But one day Buttercup made no milk, not even for Jack and his mother to drink. A few days passed and they had very little food and no money.

Jack's mother said, 'Son, you'll have to take the cow to the market in the village and sell her for as much money as you can.'

So, after tying a rope around Buttercup's neck, Jack set off. He trudged wearily along the dusty road. He hadn't gone far when he met an old man.

'On your way to the market?' asked the old man.

Jack nodded. 'I'm going to sell this cow, Buttercup.'

'Well now,' said the old man. 'I may be able to help you there. I'm looking for a cow just like this one. In exchange, I'll give you these…' and he held open a small bag.

Jack peered inside. 'Beans?' he said. 'Mother said we need money for food.'

'But these are no ordinary beans,' said the man, with a smile. 'They're magic beans.'

Jack thought for a moment. It was still a long way to market and the beans did look different from other beans and his mother would be proud that he'd brought home something special instead of just money, so he agreed. He took the bag of beans and ran home excitedly.

When his mother saw the beans she was furious. 'What have you done, you silly boy?' she shouted. 'You've sold our cow for a bag of worthless beans!' and she threw them out of the window and sent Jack to bed without any supper.

The next morning, Jack awoke early. When he looked out of the window he saw something amazing that made him forget how hungry he was. An enormous plant had sprung up from the place where his mother had thrown the beans –

a beanstalk. The beanstalk twisted and turned and stretched up into the blue sky, disappearing into the clouds. Its leaves were each almost as big as the window.

Jack wondered where the beanstalk ended, so he began to climb, higher and higher. Soon his head was in the fluffy, white clouds and he could see a path stretching ahead of him. So, leaving the beanstalk behind, he began to walk along the path.

After a while he saw a great castle. Jack realised he was hungry and thought perhaps he could ask for something to eat so he knocked on the huge wooden door.

An ugly old woman appeared. 'Aha,' she said. 'I need a boy to clean the fireplace every day. Come in quickly before my husband sees you or he'll eat you up.' And with that, she grabbed Jack's arm, dragged him inside and closed the door.

As soon as he was inside Jack felt the floor begin to shake. 'Quick,' said the ugly old woman. 'It's my husband, the giant. Hide in this cupboard.' Jack just managed to climb into the cupboard before the whole castle began to tremble.

'Fee, fi, fo, fum,
I smell the blood of an Englishman.
Be he alive or be he dead,
I'll grind his bones to make my bread!' the giant roared.

'Nonsense,' said his wife. 'It's just this ox I've roasted for your breakfast. Now hurry up and eat before it gets cold.'

So the giant sat down and soon finished his breakfast. 'Bring me my magic hen,' he shouted. 'I want to count its golden eggs.'

Jack couldn't resist peeping out of the cupboard. He saw the ugly old woman fetch a hen and set it down before the giant. 'Lay!' the giant commanded and sure enough the hen laid a beautiful golden egg. 'Lay!' he commanded again, and again the hen laid a beautiful egg of pure gold. This went on for a few minutes until the giant began to grow weary. Soon his eyes began to close and loud snores shook the walls.

Seeing his chance, Jack crept out of the cupboard, snatched up the hen and ran out of the castle as fast as his legs would carry him. He ran along the path and didn't stop until he got to the top of the beanstalk. Tucking the hen under his arm, Jack scrambled down the beanstalk and rushed into the kitchen.

'Look, Mother,' Jack cried. 'This hen lays golden eggs!'

'Silly boy!' replied his mother. 'Whoever heard of a hen that lays golden eggs?'

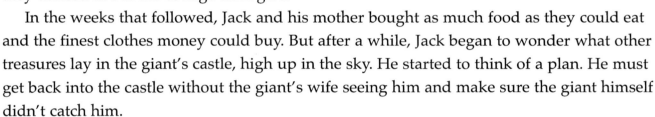

He put the hen down and said, 'Lay!' And sure enough the hen laid a golden egg.

'We shall be rich!' shouted Jack's mother and they danced about the cottage with glee.

In the weeks that followed, Jack and his mother bought as much food as they could eat and the finest clothes money could buy. But after a while, Jack began to wonder what other treasures lay in the giant's castle, high up in the sky. He started to think of a plan. He must get back into the castle without the giant's wife seeing him and make sure the giant himself didn't catch him.

So it was that one day Jack decided to go back up the enormous beanstalk. He climbed higher and higher up the twisting, turning stalks, through the huge green leaves until at last his head was above the clouds.

He peered ahead and saw the path leading to the castle in the distance. Quickly, Jack ran along the path and hammered loudly on the wooden door. As the giant's wife pulled the heavy door open, Jack flattened himself against the wall and threw a pebble to land on the path at the other side of the door. The giant's wife stepped outside. 'Who's there?' she shouted. Nimbly, Jack slipped inside – just in time – as the giant's wife shook her head and slammed the door shut.

Jack ran to the kitchen and hid in the same cupboard as before. He didn't have to wait long before the giant's footsteps thundered closer. The giant sat in his favourite chair, but then sniffed the air and shouted:

'Fee, fi, fo, fum,
I smell the blood of an Englishman.
Be he alive or be he dead,
I'll grind his bones to make my bread!'

'Nonsense,' said his wife. 'It's this cow I'm roasting for your supper.'

The giant gobbled down his supper and then demanded, 'Wife, bring me my magic harp!'

Jack listened carefully from inside the cupboard and as soon as the giant said 'Play!' Jack heard the most beautiful music flowing from the magic harp. The harp played a happy tune and the giant clapped along to the rhythm.

After a few tunes the giant grew weary. 'Play me a lullaby,' he commanded. The harp played the softest, sweetest lullaby and soon the whole room was rumbling as the giant fell asleep and began to snore.

Jack knew this was his chance. He crept out of the cupboard and grabbed the magic harp. But as he seized hold of it, it began to shriek, 'Master! Master!' and a horrible jangling noise came from its magic strings.

The giant leapt up, wide awake. With a roar he lumbered after Jack and they raced out of the castle and along the path. Jack could feel the path tremble with the giant's heavy footsteps and it seemed he was getting closer with every second. But soon Jack saw the top of the beanstalk. He tucked the magic harp under his arm and began to climb down. The giant was close behind and the beanstalk began to sway and shake as the giant climbed down after Jack. Down they climbed and down.

Almost there! Jack looked down and saw his mother far below in the garden of their cottage. 'Mother!' he shouted. 'Fetch me an axe!'

Jack climbed down with the giant right behind. He put down the harp and grabbed the axe from his mother and with all his strength swung it at the bottom of the beanstalk, just as the giant's boots came into view.

The beanstalk crashed to the ground, killing the giant instantly. And Jack and his mother lived happily ever after with the hen that lays the golden eggs and the magic harp that plays the most beautiful music ever heard.

Jack and the Beanstalk

As Jack was on his way to market he met an old man.

"I'll swap these magic beans for that old cow."

"Mother will be pleased!"

But when he got home, his mother was furious. She threw the beans out of the window and sent Jack to bed without any supper.

"You silly boy! Go straight to bed!"

The next morning, Jack saw a huge beanstalk stretching up into the sky. Curious, he began to climb up the beanstalk and found an enormous castle at the top.

"Please, do you have any food?"

"Mm, I could use a boy to do the work."

They went inside but the woman's husband, a giant, appeared and Jack had to hide.

"FEE, FI, FO, FUM, I SMELL THE BLOOD OF AN ENGLISHMAN. BE HE ALIVE, OR BE HE DEAD, I'LL GRIND HIS BONES TO MAKE MY BREAD!"

"You silly man. It's the ox I'm cooking."

When he was full, the giant asked for his hen that lays golden eggs.

"LAY!"

Soon the giant fell asleep. Jack crept out of the cupboard, snatched up the hen and then climbed down the beanstalk.

"Mother and I will be rich now!"

But after a few weeks, Jack began to wonder what other treasures the giant had in his castle. One day he climbed back up the beanstalk.

I'll knock on the door and then hide. When she opens the door I'll sneak inside.

Inside the castle, Jack quickly hid in a cupboard.

FEE, FI, FO, FUM, I SMELL THE BLOOD OF AN ENGLISHMAN. BE HE ALIVE, OR BE HE DEAD, I'LL GRIND HIS BONES TO MAKE MY BREAD!

You silly man. It's just this cow I'm roasting for supper.

After eating, the giant called for his magic harp. He commanded the harp to play and the room was filled with wonderful music.

Soothed by the music, the giant fell asleep. As soon as Jack heard him snoring he took his chance.

But the harp began to shriek. The giant awoke and chased after Jack. Jack climbed down the beanstalk, the giant close behind.

Master! Master!

Mother, fetch the axe!

Jack chopped at the beanstalk with all his strength. As the beanstalk toppled over, the giant hit his head and fell down dead.

WE'RE RICH!

TEXT 2
The Seal Wife

There once lived a young fisherman called Magnus who had a secret. At night, when the moon was full and the shore was lit by its silvery light, the seals left the sea and became seal people. They pulled off their soft sealskins and ran and danced along the shore beneath the glimmering moon. Before the harsh sun had time to rise they would pull on their skins once again and slip quietly back into the ocean.

One night, just before the full moon rose, Magnus crept out of his cottage and hid behind one of the large rocks that lay scattered across the bay. He waited, watching, and sure enough he soon saw the seals pull up onto the sand and slip out of their skins. As they danced, Magnus crept closer, staying in the shadows of the rocks. One of the seal women was the most beautiful creature Magnus had ever seen.

Soon they all began to put their sealskins back on and slide into the sea. Magnus returned to his cottage but his mind was filled with the beautiful seal woman. He thought about her until it was time for the next full moon and knew that he wanted her for his wife.

And so it was that the next time they left the sea, Magnus looked for the beautiful seal woman and watched where she left her skin. Again, as they danced along the shore, Magnus crept closer. He took the skin and hid it.

When the time came for them to go back to the sea, the beautiful woman could not find her skin. As the others slid back into the dark waves she wandered the shore, searching, crying. Soon she was alone and Magnus went to comfort her and took her to his cottage. The woman was heartbroken that she couldn't follow her people but thought Magnus was kind because he offered her a home. As she slept he went out to the hillside behind the cottage and buried the sealskin beneath a cairn of stones. He knew that without her skin she would stay with him forever.

As the weeks passed she spent hours looking out to sea. But she began to love Magnus and they became man and wife. Often he would hear her singing soft sweet songs that rose and fell like the gentle swell of the waves. On other days her songs were strange and wild like storm-tossed waves whipped by strong winds.

Wherever she wandered she would never leave the sea far behind. She wouldn't go to the village or nearby town, always wanting the sea breeze on her face and to hear the cry of the gulls. Instead she spent hours wandering along the beach, always looking, searching for the skin she could never find.

As the years passed she seemed to accept her new life and became more settled. They had five sons. Four of them were tall children with blonde hair and blue eyes. But the youngest boy was small and his hair had a silvery sheen. His eyes were as dark as the sea on a stormy night.

They all lived happily together for many years. Magnus adored his beautiful wife and was proud of their sons. The only time he worried was when he saw her staring out to sea, lost in a world he could never share with her. At those times he felt guilty about what he had done and how he had deceived her.

One day after Magnus had taken the three eldest boys fishing, the youngest two were playing on the hillside behind the cottage as usual. They were playing hide and seek, using the cairns of stones to hide behind. When it was the youngest boy's turn to hide, he noticed something hidden inside one of the cairns. Something that had a silvery sheen. He quickly lost interest in the game with his brother and began to move the stones so that he could pull out the skin. Never had he seen anything so beautiful. Never had he felt anything so soft.

Clutching it to him, he ran down the hillside to the cottage, followed by his brother, to ask his mother what the strange object was.

As soon as she saw the sealskin, the woman held it closely, rubbing her cheek against its softness and she began to weep. The two boys were worried by her strange behaviour. She ran out of the cottage and onto the shore. At the water's edge, she paused to pull on the skin. Sleek, dark heads appeared amongst the waves and the seals began to call to her. In the distance, Magnus and his three sons were returning with their catch but she paid no attention to their shouts.

She slid into the sea and as the water covered her head her eyes wept tears of joy and sadness. She thrust her sleek head above the waves and called to her youngest son who suddenly understood but had no sealskin to join her.

Magnus pleaded with her to remove the skin and stay with her family but the pull of the ocean and her people was too strong. A plaintive cry called across the waves and, with a final look at those she had learned to love, she turned away to join with her own kind once again.

Magnus and his sons never saw her again. But on calm, sunny days they sometimes heard a distant, beautiful song whisper across the waves and on storm-lashed dark nights they often heard a plaintive wail carried to shore by the harsh winds.

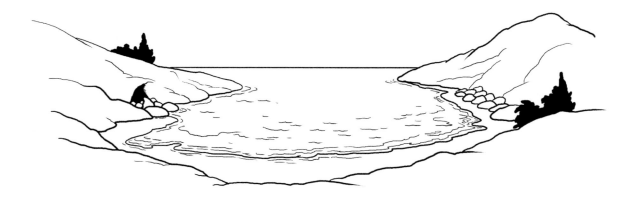

The Seal Wife

A fisherman called Magnus watched the seal people leave the sea and, after taking off their skins, dance in the moonlight.

He saw a beautiful woman and stole her skin.

She's the most beautiful woman I've ever seen. I'd like her to be my wife.

As the other seal people returned to the sea, the woman searched for her skin. As she sat sobbing by the water's edge, Magnus approached her.

I can't go with my people.

You can stay with me.

Magnus knew that the only way she would stay was if she never found her sealskin. So, while she slept, he hid it under a cairn.

Now she can never return to the sea.

As the years went by, the woman grew to love Magnus and they married. They had five sons. Four were tall and blonde but the youngest was small and dark with silvery hair.

One day, Magnus took his three eldest sons fishing.

Bye! We'll bring home a good catch!

Farewell.

TEXT 3
The Three Little Pigs

Once upon a time there were three little pigs. The three little pigs lived with the three little pigs' mother. One day, the three little pigs' mother said to the three little pigs, 'It is time for the three little pigs to go out into the big, wide world.'

So the three little pigs set off. Now these three little pigs were quite lazy little pigs. The sun blazed down and the first little pig soon grew tired. 'The first little pig is going to build his home here,' said the first little pig. The other little pigs carried on but the first little pig began to gather straw from the nearby fields.

Soon the first little pig had built the first little pig's house of straw. Then the first little pig settled down inside for a nice long snooze.

Meanwhile, the other little pigs had found a nice, leafy wood. The second little pig said, 'The second little pig will build the second little pig's house from sticks. There are plenty of sticks lying around here so collecting sticks won't take the second little pig very long. Then the second little pig can have a nice long rest.'

And so the third little pig carried on alone towards the town. The third little pig decided to build the third little pig's house from bricks. The third little pig worked and worked until darkness fell. At last the third little pig had finished and the third little pig went inside to rest.

Now all this time he had been watching them. He had seen him build it of it and he had seen him build it of them as well. And now he had seen him build it with them. All this watching had made him very hungry and he decided it was time for a feast.

So he went to his house and knocked on it. 'You, you, let me come in,' he called.

'Not by it of my chinny, chin chin,' he replied.

'Then I'll huff and I'll puff and I'll blow it down,' he said. So he huffed and he puffed and he blew it down. He ran to it but he followed him.

Again, he knocked on it. 'You, you, let me come in,' he called.

'Not by it of my chinny, chin chin,' they replied.

'Then I'll huff and I'll puff and I'll blow it down,' he said. So he huffed and he puffed and he blew it down.

Planning sheet 1

Character (Name) _____   Villain _____

Tale _____   Animal _____

Magical item _____   Setting _____

Beginning
(Describe the character and tale.)

Middle
(Magical item, animal, villain and setting.)

Problem
(Character meets villain.)

Problem solved
(How? Did the item or animal help?)

Ending
(Character successful.)

Word bank – lived, wandered, followed, arrived, searched, crept, flew, magical, suddenly, returned, hidden, stolen, fierce, dangerous, wonderful, brought, found, disappeared, beautiful, evil, wicked, giant, special, ugly

Other words I will use

Planning sheet 2

Character (Name) _____   Villain _____

Tale _____   Animal _____

Magical item _____   Setting _____

Beginning

Build-up

Problem

Problem solved

Ending

Helpful words – travelled, journey, searched, found, realised, hurried, mysterious, loathed, ancient, royal, frightened, surprised, special, secret, discovered, sinister, fierce, dangerous, magical, terrifying, incredible, approached, staggered, succeeded, returned, happily

Planning sheet 3

Character (Name) _____   Villain _____

Tale _____   Animal _____

Magical item _____   Setting _____

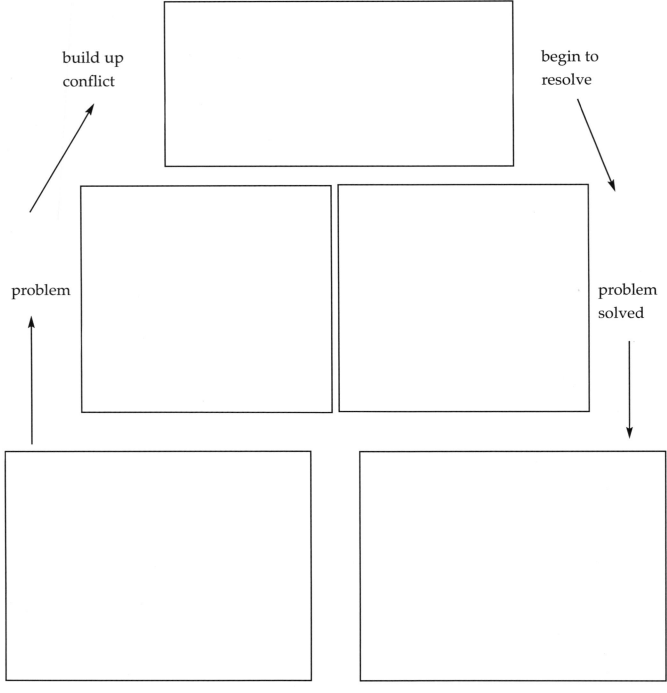